CAMBRIDGE

T0363840

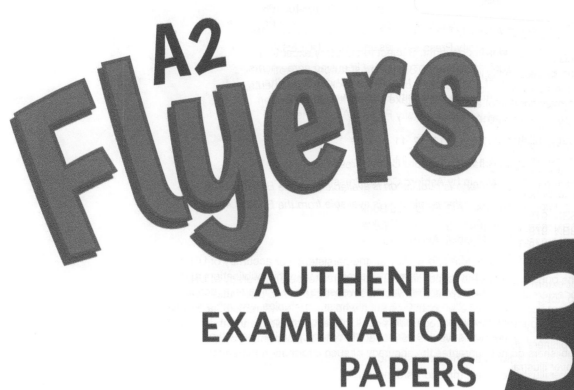

A2 Flyers

AUTHENTIC EXAMINATION PAPERS

3

STUDENT'S BOOK

Cambridge University Press
www.cambridge.org/elt

Cambridge Assessment English
www.cambridgeenglish.org

Information on this title: www.cambridge.org/9781108465168

© Cambridge University Press & Assessment and UCLES 2019

This publication is in copyright. Subject to statutory exception
and to the provisions of relevant collective licensing agreements,
no reproduction of any part may take place without the written
permission of Cambridge University Press & Assessment.

First published 2019

20 19 18 17 16 15 14 13 12 11 10 9

Printed in Great Britain by Ashford Colour Press Ltd.

A catalogue record for this publication is available from the British Library

ISBN 978-1-108-46518-8 Student's Book
ISBN 978-1-108-46520-8 Answer Booklet
ISBN 978-1-108-46526-7 Audio CD

The publisher has no responsibility for the persistence or accuracy of URLs
for external or third-party internet websites referred to in this publication, and
do not guarantee that any content on such websites is, or will remain, accurate
or appropriate. Information regarding prices, travel timetables, and other factual
information given in this work is correct at the time of first printing but the
publishers do not guarantee the accuracy of such information thereafter.

Cover illustration: Leo Trinidad/Astound

Contents

Listening

Part 1
– 5 questions –

Listen and draw lines. There is one example.

Harry   Emma   Richard   Helen

William   Oliver   Sarah

Part 2

– 5 questions –

Listen and write. There is one example.

School camping trip

Will stay for 2 nights in the: ....desert..................

1   Camp is near: .... Pyramid

2   Children must remember: ....

3   Will ride: ....

4   Meal on first evening: rice and ....

5   Name of new teacher: Miss ....

Part 3

– 5 questions –

Where did Aunt Betty buy each of these things in her cupboard?

Listen and write a letter in each box. There is one example.

the belt	B
the umbrella	☐
the necklace	☐
the crown	☐
the ring	☐
the gloves	☐

A

B

C

D

E

F

G

H

Part 4
– 5 questions –

Listen and tick (✔) the box. There is one example.

How did Michael get to the hotel?

A ✔   B ☐   C ☐

1 What did Michael have in his hotel room?

A ☐   B ☐   C ☐

2 Who stayed in Michael's room?

A ☐   B ☐   C ☐

3   What was the weather like on Friday?

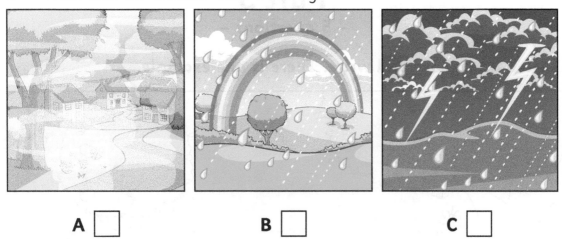

A ☐   B ☐   C ☐

4   Which food did Michael eat every day for breakfast?

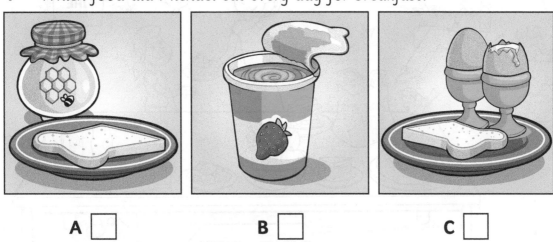

A ☐   B ☐   C ☐

5   What did Michael lose?

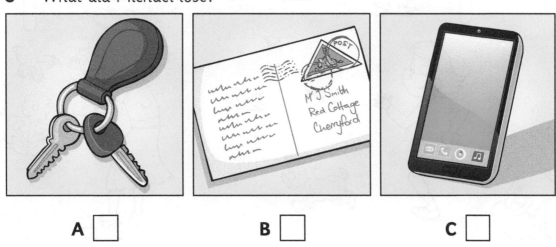

A ☐   B ☐   C ☐

Part 5

– 5 questions –

Listen and colour and write. There is one example.

Reading and Writing

Part 1

– 10 questions –

Look and read. Choose the correct words and write them on the lines. There is one example.

pyjamas   an actor   pepper   flour

This is white or brown. You use it when
you make biscuits and cakes.   ......*flour*......

1 If there is a problem with your car,
   this person can repair it.   ....

2 When you do sport, it's a good idea
   to wear these on your feet.   ....

3 This is yellow food that some people
   like to put on their bread.   ....

4 You put these on before you go to bed
   at night.   ....

5 You watch this person in films or at
   the theatre.   ....

6 This is green or black, small, and you
   can put it on pizza.   ....

7 This tastes sweet, and it is bad for
   your teeth if you eat too much.   ....

8 It is this person's job to go into space
   in a spaceship.   ....

9 These keep your hands warm when it
   is cold in winter.   ....

10 When you eat in a restaurant, this
    person will bring your food.   ....

---

an astronaut   gloves

a manager   a waiter

butter   an olive

sunglasses   trainers

a mechanic   a journalist   sugar

Part 2

– 5 questions –

George is asking his friend Holly about a club she goes to. What does Holly say?

Read the conversation and choose the best answer.
Write a letter (A–H) for each answer.

You do not need to use all the letters. There is one example.

Example

George: Hi, Holly. Are you going to go to art club today?

Holly: .... D ....

Questions

1 **George:** Do many people go to art club?

   Holly: ....

2 **George:** Do you do drawing and painting every week?

   Holly: ....

3 **George:** Have you made anything special?

   Holly: ....

4 **George:** What do you have to take with you to art club?

   Holly: ....

5 **George:** I think I'd like to join the art club.

   Holly: ....

A	Usually there are about eight of us.
B	Nothing. The teacher gives us everything we need.
C	I don't think so. I would like to be an artist.
D	Yes, I am. That's what I do every Friday. **(Example)**
E	No, we do lots of different projects.
F	Great! How about coming with me next week?
G	Yes, I designed a birthday card on the computer for my mum.
H	That's right. I'll tell the teacher.

Part 3
– 6 questions –

Read the story. Choose a word from the box. Write the correct word next to numbers 1–5. There is one example.

Example				
month	friendly	use	empty	collect
suddenly	day	instead	keep	poor

Last .... _month_ .... , when William was playing football in the

park with his dad, an enormous dog **(1)** .... appeared.

The dog was very **(2)** .... and wanted to play.

'Why are you here by yourself?' William asked the dog. 'Let's take it

home,' said Dad. 'I think someone has lost it. We might need to

(3) .... the dog for a few days. Let's try to find

out where it lives.'

William took a picture of the dog. 'I'll **(4)** ....

my computer to make some posters,' he said. He wrote 'Is this your

dog?' on them, with the picture, and his dad's phone number. Then

he put the posters on trees in the streets near his house. The next

day, a woman phoned. The dog was hers. When she came to

(5) .... it, William felt sad.

A few weeks later, William's father walked into the house. He was carrying a puppy. 'That dog we found had puppies,' said Dad. 'So I got one for you!'

(6) Now choose the best name for the story.

Tick one box.

William's dog is missing ☐

A present for Dad ☐

William gets a pet ☐

Part 4
– 10 questions –

Read the text. Choose the right words and write them on the lines.

Octopuses

Example | An octopus is a creature ....which.............. lives in the sea. It

has a round head with two large eyes. People often think that

1 | octopuses have eight legs, but they .... have

2 | four pairs of arms. Octopuses live in oceans all ....

the world. Octopuses that live in warm water are small, and

3 | .... that live in cold water are much

4 | .... Most octopuses are 'nocturnal'. This means

5 | that they sleep .... day, and move around and eat at

6 | night. Octopuses usually live .... one or two years.

To move, octopuses usually use their arms to walk

7 | .... the bottom of the sea. When they

need to, they can swim at forty kilometres an hour for a short

8 | time. .... an octopus needs to hide from

9 | .... creatures, it can change colour. It can also

get into very small spaces because its body is very soft.

10 | Octopuses are very clever. For example, they can ....

new things and open bottles. Octopuses can see very well with their

large eyes, but they can't hear anything.

Example	which	it	where
1	quite	actually	still
2	about	of	around
3	both	those	each
4	bigger	big	biggest
5	all	some	the
6	during	since	for
7	past	along	between
8	Before	If	While
9	more	every	other
10	learn	learning	learned

Part 5

– 7 questions –

Look at the picture and read the story. Write some words to complete the sentences about the story. You can use 1, 2, 3 or 4 words.

<u>The concert</u>

It was Sophia's birthday last week. Her grandfather gave her tickets for a pop concert. The concert was in a stadium. Sophia went with her mother. Mum drove them to the stadium in her car. While they were driving there, they saw a man in the road. He waved at them. Mum stopped her car. 'Do you need any help?' she asked. 'Yes, please,' said the man, 'I've got a problem with my car engine. Can you give me a lift to the stadium? I'm late for work.' 'Of course!' said Mum.

During the journey, Mum turned on the radio. She and the man chatted. Sophia didn't. She was listening to the music and thinking about the band. She was very excited about seeing them on the stage.

When they arrived at the stadium, the man said, 'Come with me, Sophia. I've got a surprise for you.' Sophia and Mum followed him. He took them behind the stage. Sophia saw the singer, and the other members of the band. Sophia talked to the band members for a few minutes and Mum took lots of photos of them. When it was time for the concert to start, a woman took Sophia and Mum to sit in the best seats at the front.

After the concert, Sophia said, 'What an amazing day!'

Examples

Sophia got tickets to see ....a pop concert......... for her birthday.

The tickets were a present from Sophia's ....grandfather......... .

Questions

1 Sophia and her mother went to the stadium by

....

2 Mum stopped because .... needed help.

3 During the drive to the stadium, Sophia thought about
.... while Mum and the man chatted.

4 Sophia felt .... about seeing the concert.

5 At the stadium, the man took Sophia and Mum
.... , where they met the band.

6 Mum .... of Sophia when she was talking
to the band.

7 Sophia and Mum watched the concert from .... ,
which were very near the stage.

Part 6

– 5 questions –

Read the postcard and write the missing words. Write one word on each line.

Example	We .... *are* .... camping in the mountains! Today, the
1	weather is horrible, but I don't mind .... it's
	warm in our tent. Every evening, my brother and I get wood for
2	a fire, then we .... a board game while Mum
3	and Dad cook dinner. There are lots of .... here,
	like butterflies and beetles. I think they're really interesting, but
	Mum doesn't like them. Tomorrow we're going to go rock climbing in
4	the mountains. I .... never climbed before. Mum
5	says it's very beautiful at the top, so I must ....
	forget to take my camera.

Part 7

Look at the three pictures. Write about this story. Write 20 or more words.

....

....

....

....

....

....

Listening

Part 1
– 5 questions –

Listen and draw lines. There is one example.

Sophia   Katy   George   Robert

Betty   David   Helen

Part 2
– 5 questions –

Listen and write. There is one example.

Cycling club

Day cycling club meets: .... Mondays ....

1 Name of William's classmate at the club: ....

2 Today children learnt about: ....

3 Place where children cycle: in park on ....

4 Children must wear: a ....

5 End of the year party with: ....

Part 3
– 5 questions –

Where did Uncle Harry take each of these photos?

Listen and write a letter in each box. There is one example.

flowers — F

a gate — ☐

a taxi — ☐

a shelf — ☐

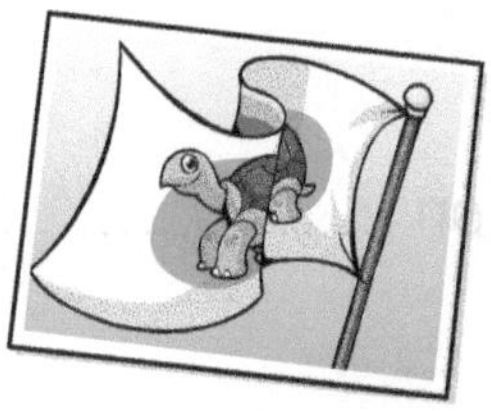

a flag — ☐

a painting — ☐

A

B

C

D

E

F

G

H

Part 4
– 5 questions –

Listen and tick (✔) the box. There is one example.

What does Mrs Silver design in her job?

A ✔   B ☐   C ☐

1   What was Mrs Silver's favourite subject at school?

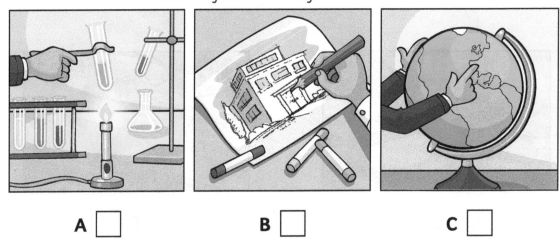

A ☐   B ☐   C ☐

2   Who else in Mrs Silver's family works as an engineer?

A ☐   B ☐   C ☐

3   What time does Mrs Silver start work?

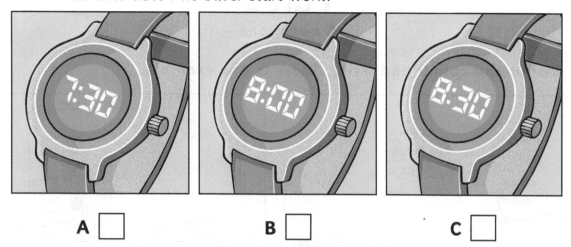

A ☐   B ☐   C ☐

4   What is Mrs Silver going to do tomorrow?

A ☐   B ☐   C ☐

5   Which bridge is Mrs Silver working on now?

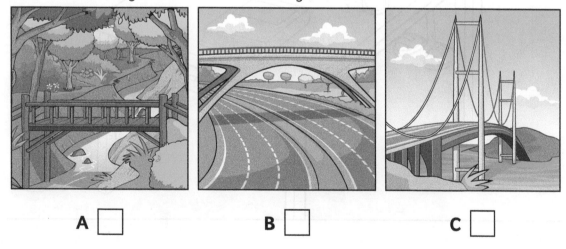

A ☐   B ☐   C ☐

Part 5

– 5 questions –

Listen and colour and write. There is one example.

Reading and Writing

Part 1

– 10 questions –

Look and read. Choose the correct words and write them on the lines. There is one example.

sugar   an astronaut   science   an engineer

history   a waiter

art   geography

a film star   olives

maths   pizza

	In this subject, you read about people who lived a long time ago.	......history......
1	This person might live in a castle and his wife might be a queen!	....
2	These are small and good to eat. They are usually green or black.	....
3	In this lesson you sometimes learn about the oceans and draw maps.	....
4	This is sweet and white. It looks like salt but doesn't taste like it!	....
5	At work, this person takes food on plates to people who are sitting in restaurants.	....
6	You may add long numbers together when you study this at school.	....
7	This hot food is often round and usually has tomatoes and cheese on the top.	....
8	This brave person travels through space in rockets or spaceships.	....
9	If you enjoy painting and drawing, this might be the best lesson on your school timetable.	....
10	This person is often very famous because he or she acts in very popular movies.	....

yoghurt   language   a king

Part 2

– 5 questions –

Oliver and Sophia are talking about an ice hockey match. What does Oliver say?

Read the conversation and choose the best answer.
Write a letter (A–H) for each answer.

You do not need to use all the letters. There is one example.

Example

Sophia: I couldn't go to the ice hockey match last night because I felt ill

Oliver: .... C ....

Questions

1 **Sophia:** Which team won the match?

Oliver: ....

2 **Sophia:** Which player scored the most goals?

Oliver: ....

3 **Sophia:** Do you think our team played well?

Oliver: ....

4 **Sophia:** What did you do after the match?

Oliver: ....

5 **Sophia:** Are you going to go to the next match too?

Oliver: ....

A Not in the first half of the game, but they improved in the second half.

B Because it was such a fast game.

C I'm pleased you're better now. **(Example)**

D I'd like to, but I don't know the date of that yet.

E At six thirty in the sports stadium.

F Ours! But it wasn't easy for them.

G We were hungry so Dad took us for a burger!

H The newest one. I can't remember his name.

Part 3
– 6 questions –

Read the story. Choose a word from the box. Write the correct word next to numbers 1–5. There is one example.

Example				
programme	friendly	texts	office	turned
borrow	guessed	important	ways	disappear

Katy was listening to her favourite music ....programme.......... on the radio when she heard something exciting! The woman said, 'Here's some **(1)** .... news! The Gold Stars' pop concert will be in City Hall next Sunday. Buy your tickets quickly! Lots of people will want to come!'

'Wow! I must tell my friends,' Katy thought. She

(2) .... on her tablet but she couldn't get online or find her phone anywhere.

'Can I **(3)** .... your phone, Mum?' she asked. 'I must send a message to all my friends!'

'Sorry,' Mum said. 'I left my phone in my **(4)** .... yesterday. Why don't you cycle to your friends' homes instead?'

'Cycle?' answered Katy.

'I had to do that when I was young!' Mum said. 'There was no internet and you couldn't use phones to send messages or find out information.'

'No wifi? No apps? No **(5)** .... ? That's terrible, Mum!' Katy said and then she laughed and ran outside and got on her racing bike.

(6) Now choose the best name for the story.

Tick one box.

Katy gets an amazing new phone ☐

Katy needs to talk to her friends ☐

Katy sings in a special concert ☐

Part 4
– 10 questions –

Read the text. Choose the right words and write them on the lines.

Camels

Example Camels have unusual shapes on their backs. These are ....<u>called</u>.................. 'humps'.

1 .... are two kinds of camel. The first kind has one

2 hump on .... back and the other kind has two humps.

3 Most camels in the world live .... the weather

is hot and dry – in places like deserts, for example. The people

4 .... also live in these places might

5 .... camels to carry all their heavy things on

6 long journeys. These people have .... camels for

thousands of years, too.

Camels can live without food or water for six months and most camels

7 live .... forty and fifty years! About fourteen

million camels live in the world at the moment.

8 It is easier for camels to live in deserts ....for

other animals because their bodies are high above the hot ground and

9 their large feet help them .... quickly across sand.

10 A camel can run across sand really fast. ....

camels can travel 45 kilometres in one hour.

Example	call	calling	called
1	They	There	Those
2	your	my	its
3	where	when	why
4	who	what	which
5	used	use	using
6	ride	rode	ridden
7	during	between	until
8	than	while	if
9	moved	moving	move
10	Many	Lots	Much

Part 5
– 7 questions –

Look at the picture and read the story. Write some words to complete the sentences about the story. You can use 1, 2, 3 or 4 words.

David's Dream

David often had dreams about adventures in dangerous places. Last Sunday night, he had a really fantastic dream.

He was climbing a mountain. He was so high, there were clouds below him. Above him, he saw an eagle's nest in a hole in the rock. There were two white eggs inside. David didn't touch them, but when his right hand was near to the nest, an eagle appeared. Its wings were enormous. That was scary!

Then David saw the entrance to a really deep, dark cave. He moved carefully and quietly past it but then a huge brown bear jumped out and made a frightening noise. David hurried up the mountain. That bear had big teeth and very strong legs.

When David got to the top of the mountain, he saw some grass and lay down on it. He was really tired and was soon asleep. Then he heard someone say, 'Wake up, David. Wake up!'

David opened his eyes and saw his mother.

'I had another amazing dream about a mountain, Mum,' he said.

'That's strange!' David's mother answered. 'Because it's the first day of your summer holidays today and we're going to do something very special.'

'What?' asked David.

'We're going to go on a trip!'

'Where to?' asked David.

'The mountains! Dad says we might see an eagle!'

'And a bear?' David laughed.

Examples

David's ....dreams............ were often about adventures in dangerous places.

David had a really amazing dream last ....Sunday night.......... .

Questions

1   In his dream, David climbed a mountain that was really

    ....

2   In the eagle's nest David found ....

3   When his .... was next to the nest, David saw
    the enormous eagle.

4   Then David climbed past a .... that looked
    really dark.

5   David felt afraid when a .... made a horrible
    sound.

6   David lay down on .... when he got to the top
    of the mountain.

7   Then David woke up and his .... told him about
    their special trip to the mountains!

Part 6
– 5 questions –

Read the diary and write the missing words. Write one word on each line.

Example	It snowed last night! I .... was .... so surprised when
	I got up and looked outside!
1	Mum and I mixed some flour, eggs and milk ....
	make pancakes for our breakfast. They tasted really delicious!
2	I had six. Mum had four. Then I .... on my new
	warm gloves and I went and got our old sledge. My little brother
3	.... down on it and then I pulled him to
4	the park! Our friends, Harry and Michael, ...
	already there with their snowboards. We had such a lot
5	...................................fun. We didn't want to come home!

Part 7

Look at the three pictures. Write about this story. Write 20 or more words.

....

....

....

....

....

Listening

Part 1
– 5 questions –

Listen and draw lines. There is one example.

George   Sarah   David   Katy

Harry   Helen   Sophia

Part 2
– 5 questions –

Listen and write. There is one example.

<u>Visiting Grandpa</u>

When: .... next weekend ....

1	Other child at Grandpa's:	Emma, his ....
2	Meet Grandpa in car park outside the:	....
3	Animals they will see at the museum:	some ....
4	Name of museum:	The .... Museum
5	Day to visit museum:	....

Part 3

– 5 questions –

Where did Holly and her friends find each of these presents at the birthday party?

Listen and write a letter in each box. There is one example.

	the bracelet	G
	the puzzle	☐
	the ring	☐
	the necklace	☐
	the diary	☐
	the chess game	☐

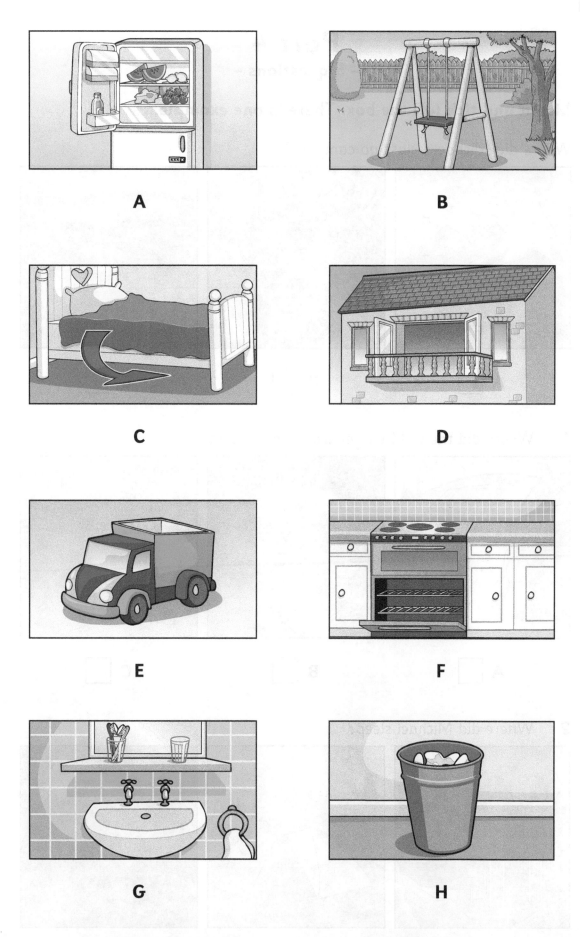

A

B

C

D

E

F

G

H

Part 4
– 5 questions –

Listen and tick (✔) the box. There is one example.

Where did Michael's class go camping?

A ✔   B ☐   C ☐

1   Where did the children get water for washing?

A ☐   B ☐   C ☐

2   Where did Michael sleep?

A ☐   B ☐   C ☐

3 What job did Michael do?

A ☐   B ☐   C ☐

4 What did Michael have for dinner on the first night?

A ☐   B ☐   C ☐

5 How did Michael send a message to his parents?

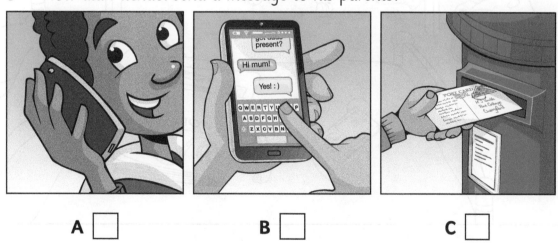

A ☐   B ☐   C ☐

Part 5

– 5 questions –

Listen and colour and write. There is one example.

Reading and Writing

Part 1

– 10 questions –

Look and read. Choose the correct words and write them on the lines. There is one example.

honey   a fire engine   a bicycle   cereal

Bees make this sweet food, which some
people put in their tea.   ....honey....

1   You often need this to open the door to
    your house.   ....

an ambulance   a gate

2   People sometimes use this if they don't
    have a car. The driver takes them where
    they want to go.   ....

3   These are soft and people put them on
    their sofas or beds.   ....

jam   a motorway

4   These are usually made of wood or
    plastic. You hold two in one hand to eat
    rice or noodles.   ....

5   This has two wheels. You should wear a
    helmet when you ride this.   ....

6   You must be careful if you use this to
a key   make hot food because it can burn you.   ....   chopsticks

7   If you are very ill and you need to go to
    the hospital quickly, you can go in this.   ....

8   You can use strawberries or other fruit
    to make this food. You can have it on
a cooker   bread with butter.   ....   shelves

9   This is a kind of road where you can
    drive fast.   ....

10 Many people like this for breakfast, and
    use a bowl and spoon to eat it with milk.   ....

---

cushions   knives   a taxi

Part 2
– 5 questions –

Emma is talking to Oliver about camping. What does Oliver say?

Read the conversation and choose the best answer.
Write a letter (A–H) for each answer.

You do not need to use all the letters. There is one example.

Example

Emma: Did your parents take you camping this summer?

Oliver: .... D ....

Questions

1 **Emma:** How long did you camp for?

Oliver: ....

2 **Emma:** What fun things did you do?

Oliver: ....

3 **Emma:** Who cooked the meals?

Oliver: ....

4 **Emma:** Did you like sleeping in a tent?

Oliver: ....

5 **Emma:** What time did you wake up in the mornings?

Oliver: ....

A   Not me! But I helped with other things.

B   No, we didn't know anyone else. But people were friendly.

C   A lot of fishing. And we went for walks at night with a torch.

D   Yes, it was great. We went to the same place last year, too.
      (Example)

E   Quite early, because the birds were noisy and there was so much
      to do!

F   My backpack was very heavy and I had to carry it by myself.

G   This year was unusual because we went for a month!

H   It was really cool. But in the morning there were insects in my
      shoes!

Part 3
– 6 questions –

Read the story. Choose a word from the box. Write the correct word next to numbers 1–5. There is one example.

Example				
path	remember	away	hurrying	instead
selling	smell	scissors	cheap	pleased

One day, Harry and his dad went to the park. It was sunny and there were

lots of flowers along the ....path.............. where they were walking.

'These flowers look and **(1)** .... wonderful. How about

taking some home?' said Harry. 'We mustn't do that!' said Dad. 'These

flowers are for everyone to enjoy. But I've got an idea!'

Dad and Harry went to a market and found a person who was

(2) .... plants. They chose some, brought them home

and put them in the garden in front of the house. Harry watered them every

day. When flowers started to appear, Harry was really

(3) .... Everyone who saw them smiled.

One day, Harry saw Dad with some **(4)** .... in his

hand. 'I'm going to cut some flowers to put on the kitchen table.'

'No! You mustn't! They're for everyone to enjoy! Don't you

(5) .... ?' said Harry with a smile. 'Of course,

you're right!' said Dad.

(6) Now choose the best name for the story.

Tick one box.

Dad's job in the park ☐

The expensive plants ☐

Harry's beautiful flowers ☐

Part 4
– 10 questions –

Read the text. Choose the right words and write them on the lines.

Skyscrapers

Example Many large cities ....in.............. the world have

skyscrapers. In the past, a 'skyscraper' was a kind of high sail

on a sailing ship. But today the word 'skyscraper' means a very

1 .... building. Some people think that a building

2 can only be .... a skyscraper when it has more

3 than 50 floors, but others do .... agree.

4 A long time .... , buildings were usually only

five or six floors high. Then, in 1852, Elisha Otis, a mechanic,

5 invented a lift .... was safe and could carry

passengers up and down many floors. At the same time, engineers were

6 .... stronger and lighter kinds of metal. With these

7 lifts and metals, engineers could .... very high

skyscrapers for people to live and work in.

Many people think that skyscrapers are ugly because they look

8 .... big boxes.

9 But the .... famous ones have interesting shapes

10 and colours. Also, ... the top floors of skyscrapers

you can see amazing views!

Example	in	of	from
1	tallest	taller	tall
2	calling	called	call
3	not	no	never
4	since	ago	already
5	what	where	which
6	make	making	made
7	designing	designed	design
8	so	as	like
9	another	most	much
10	through	from	with

Part 5
– 7 questions –

Look at the picture and read the story. Write some words to complete the sentences about the story. You can use 1, 2, 3 or 4 words.

<u>Katy's homework</u>

Katy's class was studying the oceans, and her teacher asked them each to do an art project for homework. Katy loved art and her favourite animal was the octopus, so she decided to make a model of one. She didn't know the best way to do it, so she went online and found some information about models. Soon she was ready to start her project.

First, she mixed glue and water together in a big plastic bowl. Then she found some newspaper in the living room and she put small pieces of it into the bowl. Next, she got one round balloon and eight long ones to make the body. She lifted the wet paper out of the bowl, and put each piece around the balloons. After that, she put it by a window to dry. When it was ready, she painted it.

'Your octopus is brilliant!' said Grandpa, 'but I don't think I can read my newspaper now.' He laughed.

'Oh no! I used your newspaper! I'm sorry!' Katy said. Grandpa wanted to go to the shop to get another one, but Katy had a different idea. She went upstairs and got the laptop. 'Look,' she said. 'All the news is on these websites.' 'That's wonderful!' said Grandpa.

They both learned something new today!

Examples

Katy's class was learning about the ....oceans............... .

Katy had to do an ....art project...........for her homework.

Questions

1   For her project Katy wanted to .... of an octopus, which was her favourite animal.

2   Before she started her project, Katy needed to get
    .... online.

3   Katy put newspaper, glue and water into a ....

4   Then, Katy put the wet newspaper around some
    .... to make the body of the octopus.

5   The model dried near a window and then Katy
    .... it.

6   Katy was .... when she found out that she used Grandpa's newspaper.

7   Katy showed Grandpa some .... where he could read the news.

Part 6

– 5 questions –

Read the email and write the missing words. Write one word on each line.

	Dear Aunt Betty,
Example	Thank you ....for............. my birthday card and money.
	It was very kind of you.
1	I .... the money on a fantastic pair of trainers
	because I have just entered a running race and I want to win!
	I haven't been in a competition before – this will
2	.... my first one! I'm very excited but
3	also .... bit frightened.
4	.... you like to come and watch? Mum says
5	she can .... you there in her new car. The
	races are on Tuesday at the park.
	Thanks again!
	From Frank

Part 7

Look at the three pictures. Write about this story. Write **20** or more words.

....

....

....

....

....

....

Blank Page

Blank Page

Examiner's copy

Find the Differences

Candidate's copy

Find the Differences

Information Exchange

Examiner's copy

Daisy's art class

teacher's name	Mr Black
how many students	8
when	Friday
what / like painting	animals
good artist	not bad

John's art class

teacher's name	?
how many students	?
when	?
what / like painting	?
good artist	?

Candidate's copy

Information Exchange

Daisy's art class

teacher's name	?
how many students	?
when	?
what / like painting	?
good artist	?

John's art class

teacher's name	Miss Bird
how many students	10
when	Saturday
what / like painting	people
good artist	very good

Examiner's and Candidate's copy

Picture Story

Vicky's strange day

Vicky   Mum

Blank Page

Examiner's copy

Find the Differences

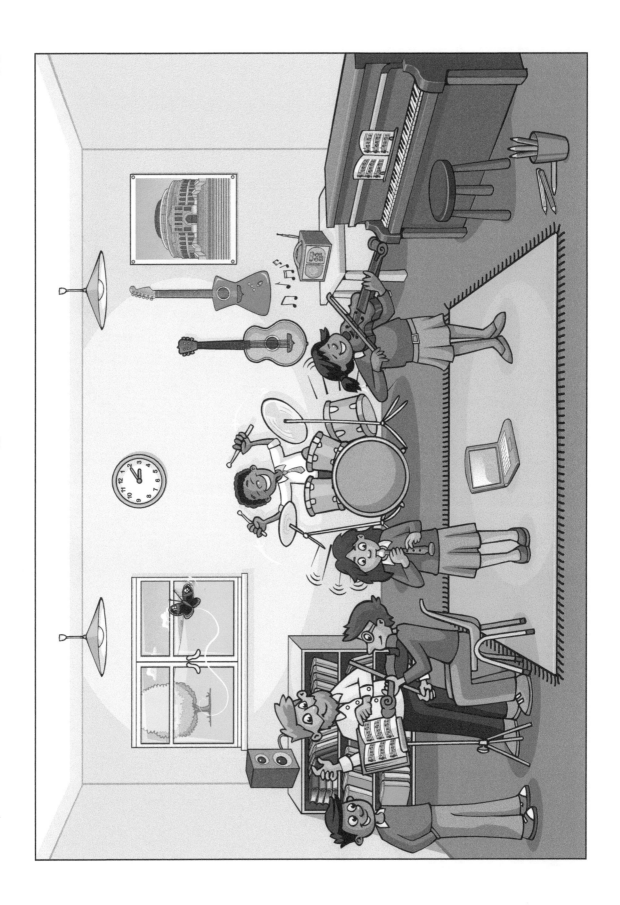

Candidate's copy

Find the Differences

Information Exchange

Robert's mum's car

colour	black
how many doors	5
age	6 months
cheap / expensive	expensive
where / now	at the station

Katy's mum's car

colour	?
how many doors	?
age	?
cheap / expensive	?
where / now	?

Information Exchange

Katy's mum's car

colour	silver
how many doors	3
age	2 years
cheap / expensive	cheap
where / now	at home

Robert's mum's car

colour	?
how many doors	?
age	?
cheap / expensive	?
where / now	?

Examiner's and Candidate's copy

Picture Story

The goat and the coconuts

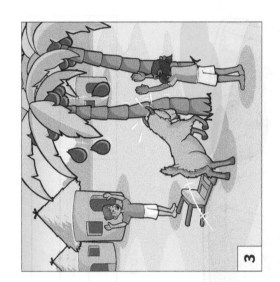

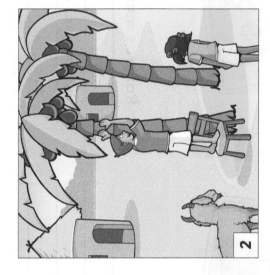

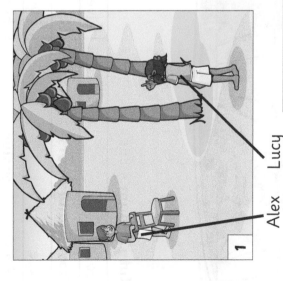

Alex   Lucy

Blank Page

Examiner's copy

Find the Differences

Candidate's copy

Find the Differences

Information Exchange

Examiner's copy

Emma's apartment

where	River Road
which floor	5th
how many bedrooms	4
colour / kitchen	yellow
balcony	no

Robert's apartment

where	?
which floor	?
how many bedrooms	?
colour / kitchen	?
balcony	?

Candidate's copy

Information Exchange

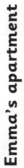

Emma's apartment

where	?
which floor	?
how many bedrooms	?
colour / kitchen	?
balcony	?

Robert's apartment

where	Winter Street
which floor	4th
how many bedrooms	3
colour / kitchen	blue
balcony	yes

Picture Story

Examiner's and Candidate's copy

A frog goes to school

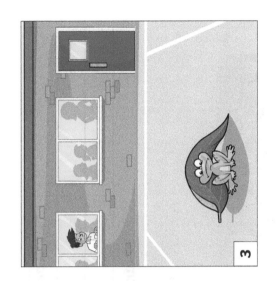

Charlie

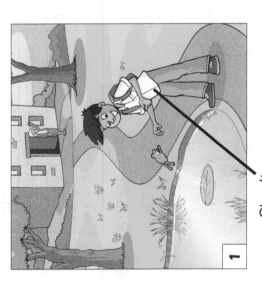

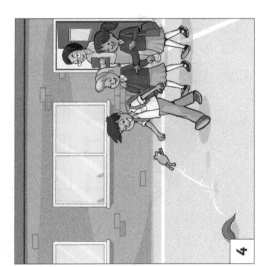

Blank Page

Blank Page

Blank Page